Incredible Reptiles

John Townsend

www.raintreepublishers.co.uk
Visit our website to find out more information about **Raintree** books.

To order:
☎ Phone 44 (0) 1865 888113
▤ Send a fax to 44 (0) 1865 314091
▣ Visit the Raintree Bookshop at **www.raintreepublishers.co.uk** to browse our catalogue and order online.

First published in Great Britain by Raintree Publishers, Halley Court, Jordan Hill, Oxford, OX2 8EJ, part of Harcourt Education Ltd.
Raintree is a registered trademark of Harcourt Education Ltd.

Produced for Raintree Publishers by Discovery Books Ltd
Editorial: Louise Galpine, Sarah Jameson, Charlotte Guillain, and Diyan Leake
Expert Reader: Jill Bailey
Design: Victoria Bevan, Keith Williams (sprout.uk.com Limited), and Michelle Lisseter
Picture Research: Maria Joannou
Production: Duncan Gilbert and Jonathan Smith
Printed and bound in China by South China Printing Company
Originated by Repro Multi Warna

ISBN 1 844 43477 X (hardback)
09 08 07 06 05
10 9 8 7 6 5 4 3 2 1

ISBN 1 844 43585 7 (paperback)
09 08 07 06 05
10 9 8 7 6 5 4 3 2 1

British Library Cataloguing in Publication Data
Townsend, John
Incredible Reptiles. – (Incredible Creatures)
597.9
A full catalogue record for this book is available from the British Library.

This levelled text is a version of Freestyle: Incredible creatures: Incredible reptiles.

Photo acknowledgements
Ardea p. 42 (Ferrero-Labat); Bruce Coleman Collection pp. 30–1 (Fred Bruemmer); Corbis pp. 10 (Theo Allofs), 16 (George Mccarthy), 46–7 (Nik Wheeler), 49 (David A. Northcott), 50 left (Bill Ross); Digital Vision p. 11 right; FLPA pp. 4–5 (Minden Pictures), 8 (C. Carvalho), 12 (Derek Middleton), 13 (Derek Middleton), 14 (Brian Turner), 17 (E. & D. Hosking), 19 (Minden Pictures), 20 (Yossi Eshbol), 20–1 (Minden Pictures), 26 (Minden Pictures), 27 right (Chris Mattison), 29 top (Winfried Wisniewski), 31 top (Fritz Polking), 34–5 (E. & D. Hosking), 39 bottom (S. C. Brown), 48 (Neil Bowman), 51 right; Gondwana Studios p. 41 inset; Naturepl pp. 6–7, 34 (Lynn M. Stone), 44 (Hanne & Jens Erikson); NHPA pp. 4 (Kevin Schaffer), 5 bottom (Anthony Bannister), 5 middle (John Shaw), 5 top, 7 (Daniel Heuclin), 8–9 (Nigel J. Dennis), 9 (Daniel Heuclin), 11 left (Martin Harvey), 12–13 (Ant Photo Library), 14–15 (Earl Switak), 15 (E. Hanumantha Rao), 16–17 (Ant Photo Library), 18 (Stephen Dalton), 18–19 (James Warwick), 21 (Pete Atkinson), 22 (Stephen Dalton), 23 left (Daniel Heuclin), 23 right (Anthony Bannister), 24 (Daniel Heuclin), 24–5 (Ant Photo Library), 25 (James Carmichael Jr), 26–7 (Martin Wendler), 28–9 (John Shaw), 32 (Jany Sauvanet), 32–3 (Anthony Bannister), 35 (Anthony Bannister), 36 (Stephen Dalton), 37 right (Anthony Bannister), 38 top (Anthony Bannister), 38 bottom (Dave Watts), 39 (James Carmichael Jr), 40 (Bruce Beehler), 40–1, 43 (K. Ghani), 44–5, 45 (Daniel Heuclin), 46 left (David Middleton); Oxford Scientific Films pp. 30, 33 (Zig Leszczynski/Animals Animals), 47 (Juan M. Renjifo), 50–1; Photodisc p. 6; Rex Features p. 28 left
Cover photograph of a chameleon reproduced with permission of FLPA (Frans Lanting/Minden Pictures)

The Publishers would like to thank Jon Pearce for his assistance in the preparation of this book. Every effort has been made to contact copyright holders of any material reproduced in this book. Any omissions will be rectified in subsequent printings if notice is given to the Publishers.

Contents

Any words appearing in the text in bold, **like this**, are explained in the Glossary. You can also look out for some of them in the 'Wild words' bank at the bottom of each page.

The world of reptiles

Did you know that reptiles have lived on Earth for over 250 million years?

Reptiles are **vertebrates**, which means they have a backbone. They are **cold-blooded** and do not make their own body heat like we do. They use heat from their surroundings to keep warm. Their skin is covered in hard plates, called **scales**.

Incredible reptiles

- The word **"dinosaur"** means "terrible lizard". Dinosaurs and birds probably both **evolved** from a kind of reptile-bird creature.

- The tuatara (below) has hardly changed in more than 200 million years!

Wild words   **scales** small, horny, or bony plates that protect the skin on reptiles and fish

All sorts

Today there are almost 6000 different **species**, or types, of reptile.

There are four main groups of reptile. Each group includes some incredible animals:

- turtles, tortoises, and terrapins
- crocodiles, alligators, caimans, and gharials (**crocodilians**)
- snakes and lizards
- tuataras, which look rather like lizards.

Find out later...

... how this reptile can walk on water.

... which reptile eats the most people.

... how fast this deadly snake can move.

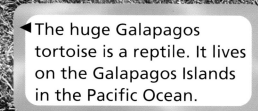

◄ The huge Galapagos tortoise is a reptile. It lives on the Galapagos Islands in the Pacific Ocean.

evolve change very slowly over time

Meet the family

One of the things that makes reptiles special is their skin. It is covered in **scales**. Many lizards and snakes have small scales that overlap. Turtle shells are made from large, solid plates that are very strong. The big, bony scales on the back of a large crocodile can even be bullet-proof!

Lizards and snakes often have to **shed** their scaly skin as they grow.

Scaly skin

Reptile scales are made from a material that is quite like our fingernails. Scales may be smooth and silky, or rough like sandpaper.

shed get rid of, or lose

Chilly blood

Reptiles are **cold-blooded**. This means they have to warm up their bodies before they will work properly. Reptiles do this by lying, or **basking**, in the sunshine.

Unlike reptiles, we use energy from the food we eat to keep our bodies warm. Unlike reptiles, we do not need the warmth of the sun to make our bodies work.

Cold and heat

Too much sun can make reptiles overheat. The rhinoceros iguana (below) can make the colour of its skin lighter in the hot sun. This reflects more heat.

◄ This python is shedding its scaly skin. Even its eyelids peel off.

cold-blooded having a body temperature that depends on the temperature of the surroundings

Reptiles with shells

There are about 250 **species** of turtle, tortoise, and terrapin. They are easy to spot because they carry a hard shell on their back.

A land tortoise often has a high, rounded shell that is difficult for **predators** to bite. A sea turtle has a flatter shell. This makes it easier for it to slip through the water.

Massive tortoise

The Aldabra tortoise (below) is big. A male can weigh up to 250 kilograms (over 550 pounds). That's as heavy as three adult men! Its shell can grow as big as the bonnet of a car.

► A leopard tortoise plods across the desert in Africa. It gets its name from the black and white patterns on its shell.

species type of living animal or plant

Turtles

Turtles live in water. There are about 200 species of turtle that live in rivers and seven types of sea turtle.

Turtles can stay under water for nearly an hour before coming up to the surface for air.

The largest sea turtle is the leatherback. It can weigh nearly as much as a small car!

Snapper

The snapping turtle (below) has sharp jaws and a large mouth. In 1999 in Ohio, USA, a snapping turtle bit off the big toe of a nine-year-old boy who was swimming in a stream.

predator animal that kills and eats other animals

Crocodilians

Crocodiles, alligators, caimans, and gharials live in rivers, lakes, and swamps. Some swim in the sea. All have thick, scaly skin. **Crocodilians** have strong jaws. They are fierce **predators**.

Longest crocodile

The biggest crocodilian is the saltwater crocodile. It can grow to be 9 metres (nearly 30 feet) long – that is nearly the length of three cars!

Caimans

Caimans (shown below) are like small alligators. They have short snouts and bony ridges around their eyes. The black caiman of South America can grow to over 4 metres (13 feet) long.

predator animal that kills and eats other animals

Alligator or crocodile?

How do you tell a crocodile from an alligator?

- Crocodiles have a more pointed **snout**.
- When crocodiles close their mouth their teeth stick up from the bottom jaw. Alligators' teeth are hidden when their mouth is closed.
- Crocodiles live in southern parts of the world, such as Africa, South America, and South-East Asia. Alligators live only in China and South, Central, and North America.

Gharials

Gharials have a long, narrow snout and very sharp teeth, which they use to catch fish.

◀ A female Nile crocodile guards her nest.

Lizards

There are more than 3700 different **species** of lizard. They live almost everywhere except places that are freezing cold. They come in all sorts of shapes, sizes, and colours.

Lizards usually have a large mouth, four legs, and a long tail. Lizard skin is covered in **scales**. These can be smooth, bumpy, or spiky.

Most common

The common lizard (below) lives in Europe and northern Asia. It is the only reptile living in Ireland. It grows to the length of a writing pen.

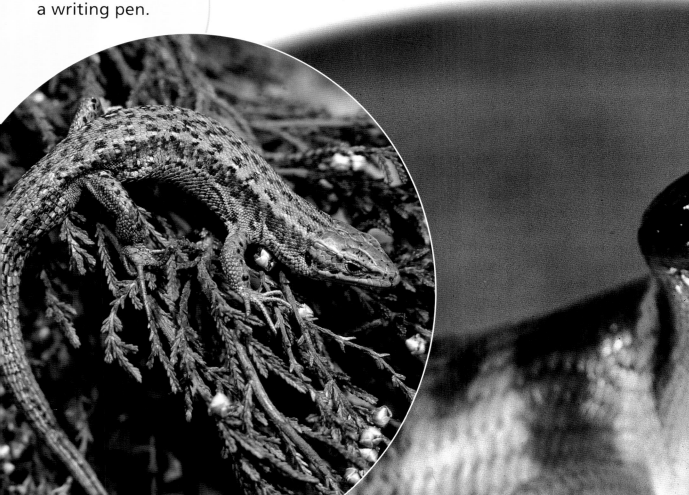

species type of living animal or plant

Skinks and dragons

Nearly one third of all lizards are skinks. These lizards often have smooth, shiny scales. Some have no legs and **burrow** in the soil.

The largest lizard is the scary Komodo dragon. It lives in South-East Asia. It can weigh almost as much as two adult men! It hunts animals as large as deer.

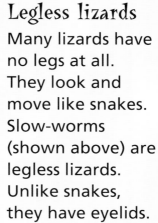

Legless lizards

Many lizards have no legs at all. They look and move like snakes. Slow-worms (shown above) are legless lizards. Unlike snakes, they have eyelids.

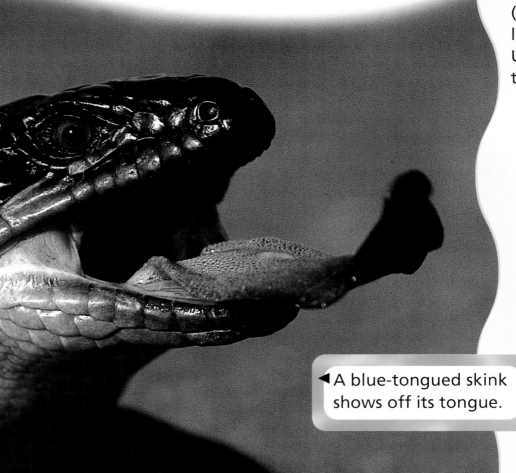

◀ A blue-tongued skink shows off its tongue.

Snakes

There are nearly 2400 **species** of snake. Although snakes have no legs, they can move in many different ways. Some snakes slither along the ground, some swim. Other snakes **burrow** in the soil. Some climb trees.

Some snakes are just a few centimetres long. The world's longest snake is the reticulated python. It can reach a length of nearly 11 metres (36 feet) – about as long as a double-decker bus!

Did you know?

• There are 20 different poisonous snakes in the USA. All states have at least one of them, apart from Maine, Alaska, and Hawaii.

• Adders or vipers (shown below) live in northern countries like the UK and in Europe. The adder is the UK's only poisonous reptile.

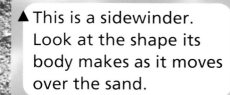

▲ This is a sidewinder. Look at the shape its body makes as it moves over the sand.

        burrow make a hole in the ground

Fast movers

The fastest land snake is the black mamba of Africa. It can reach top speeds of 19 kilometres (12 miles) per hour. That's moving!

The sidewinder desert rattlesnake lives in North America. It moves sideways over the hot sand. It arches and coils its body as it moves along, so it touches the ground as little as possible. It is a bit like us walking on our tiptoes.

King cobras

The king cobra (shown below) is the longest poisonous snake. It kills and eats other snakes. If it is scared, it can lift up the front of its body so it stands almost as tall as a human!

Rat threat

Today, tuataras only live on islands where there are no rats. This is because rats eat tuatara eggs. They also eat a lot of insects, leaving the tuatara short of food.

Tuataras

The tuatara is one of the oldest reptiles in the world today. It is the only **survivor** from a group of reptiles that lived on Earth over 200 million years ago.

There are just two **species** of tuatara. They both live on islands off New Zealand.

survivor someone or something that has stayed alive

On guard

Tuataras live in holes in the ground. Adults come out at night when there are fewer **predators** around. They eat mainly insects, but sometimes munch a small lizard or bird's egg.

Young tuataras are more active in the daytime. They do this to keep away from the adult tuataras, who sometimes try to eat them!

Cool age

Tuataras grow slowly and may live for over 100 years! Compared to other reptiles, they can live in quite cold temperatures.

◄ The tuatara looks very much like a lizard, but it is not.

Amazing bodies

Lung power

A snake's long, thin body does not have much room for two lungs. Its left lung is smaller than the right, or even missing altogether. This swimming grass snake is coming up for air.

All animals need **oxygen** to live. Like us, reptiles use lungs to breathe.

Sea breathing

Sea snakes, sea turtles, and many **crocodilians** spend a lot of their lives in water. They do not have **gills** like fish do to breathe in water. Some sea turtles take in oxygen through the insides of their mouths. Some sea snakes do the same through their skin.

▲ This is a spectacled caiman. Most of its body is under water, except for its eyes (to look for food) and its **snout** (to breathe).

oxygen one of the gases in air and water that all living things need

Deep breaths

Crocodilians spend a lot of time in water. They lie in wait for their **prey** near the water's surface. They breathe through their nostrils, which stick up above the water.

When crocodilians dive, they can hold their breath for up to an hour. They have a flap of skin at the back of their throat. This stops water going into their lungs when they are under water.

Under water

When a crocodile dives it can stop blood going to its lungs, which do not work under water. Instead, the blood goes to the crocodile's hard-working muscles.

▼ Saltwater crocodiles can swim long distances under water.

gills delicate, feathery structures that allow some animals to breathe under water

Amazing lungs

Sea turtles live most of their lives in water. They die if they spend more than a few hours on land.

Sea turtles often sleep on the seabed. They do not breathe while they sleep. Every now and then they swim up to the surface to gulp air. Then they go back down to sleep some more.

Terrapins

Some turtles live in rivers, lakes, or streams rather than the sea. These turtles are usually called terrapins. Some people keep terrapins as pets.

▶ This marine iguana uses its strong tail as a paddle to swim.

Lizards under water

The **marine** iguana is the world's only sea lizard. It lives on the Galapagos Islands in the Pacific Ocean.

Marine iguanas eat seaweed. They usually dive for just a few minutes at a time, although there are records of these lizards spending up to 45 minutes under water. After swimming they return to the land to lie in the sun and warm up.

Snakes of the sea

Over 70 **species** of snakes live in the sea. The banded sea snake (below) has to swim to the surface every two hours to breathe air. Some snakes can stay under for up to eight hours!

marine to do with the sea

Feeding

Snap it up!

When a chameleon spots a tasty insect, it creeps slowly towards it. Suddenly, it shoots out its long, sticky tongue. The insect sticks to the tongue. The chameleon then snaps its tongue – and the insect – back into its mouth.

Most reptiles are **carnivores**. This means they eat other animals, called **prey**. Most tortoises are **herbivores** and only eat plants. Some reptiles eat both.

Reptile food

Reptiles are **cold-blooded** and do not need lots of food to keep warm. Some may go for weeks without eating.

Stone swallowers

Did you know that crocodiles swallow small pebbles? The stones help grind up the tough food they have eaten.

◄ Chameleons are a type of lizard. Their tongues can be as long as their bodies!

22   Wild words   **cold-blooded** having a body temperature that depends on the temperature of the surroundings

Finding prey

How do reptiles find their food? Some go out looking for it. Others sit and wait.

Crocodilians and some large snakes hide under water. When prey comes along, they attack with amazing speed and power.

Some snakes hang from branches and wait. They flick out their tongues to "taste" the air. They can smell prey this way.

Croc teeth

Crocodilians grow hundreds of teeth during their lives. When their teeth fall out, they just grow new ones. They use their teeth to grip their food, but they cannot chew like we do.

◄ This green rat snake is 'tasting' the air.

Food for snakes

Snakes use their teeth to hold on to **prey** and stop it escaping. Some snakes kill their prey with poison. Others squeeze their prey to death.

Eggs and small animals like mice, are tasty food for many snakes. Amazingly, large snakes can eat prey as big as a deer! Snakes cannot chew their food, so how do they eat it?

Squash and gulp

Most lizards have little pointed teeth. Like snakes, they cannot chew up their food. So they squash it first in their mouth, then gulp it down whole.

▲ Juicy insects are often on the menu for green lizards.

Open wide

Snakes have **flexible** jaws, which they can open very wide. After catching their prey, they swallow it whole. A large meal can take several hours to swallow.

No teeth

Most reptiles have teeth, but turtles and tortoises do not. Instead they bite with the sharp, bony edge of their mouth.

Suck and slurp

The matamata turtle (shown below) comes from the River Amazon in South America. It lies in wait for fish and opens its mouth wide. It sucks in its food like a vacuum cleaner!

▲ The perentie is the largest monitor lizard in Australia. This one is waiting by a rabbit hole, to catch some food.

flexible able to move or bend very easily

Water from food

Lizards do not often drink water from ponds or streams. So where do they find water? They get most of the water they need from their food.

Squeezing tight

Anacondas are members of the boa constrictor family of snakes. They kill their **prey** by winding their long bodies around it. Then they squeeze really tight. The prey cannot breathe and dies. The snake then eats the animal whole.

Anacondas catch caimans, deer, and even jaguars in this way.

► This is an anaconda. It has caught a caiman and is squeezing it to death.

digestion breaking down food in the body after eating

Reptile digestion

The surrounding temperature affects the **digestion** of **cold-blooded** reptiles. Crocodiles do not like to eat when it is colder than 22 °C (71 °F), because their bodies slow down.

If a snake is too cool after feeding, it cannot **digest** its food. It has to bring the food back up again. If it does not, the food will rot in its stomach and kill it.

It may take a snake up to two weeks to digest a large meal.

Strong stomachs

How do large snakes and **crocodilians** digest whole prey? These reptiles have very strong **acids** in their stomachs. These acids eat through the bones and skin of tough prey like caimans or buffalo.

▼ The Australian amethystine python will only attack small prey.

acid type of liquid that can be strong enough to break down tough materials

Salties

The saltwater crocodile is the biggest reptile around. It is one of the most powerful animals on Earth. Some can weigh as much as a tonne (2000 pounds).

Saltwater crocodiles live in South-East Asia and Australia. They can live far out to sea, but they are also at home in rivers and lakes inland.

These crocodiles feed at night. They kill and eat a variety of animals, birds, and fish.

Crocodile attack!

Saltwater crocodiles attack and kill more people than any other reptile. Even crocodile hunters like Steve Irwin (below) have to be very careful when close to these reptiles.

Alligator trouble

In 1999 in Rio de Janeiro, South America, some builders scared a large alligator from its home. Feeling hungry, the alligator walked into a backyard. It ate the owner's dog and four chickens.

The city is spreading into the places where alligators live. It is bringing these reptiles closer to where people live.

Big eaters

Nile crocodiles live all over Africa, not just in the River Nile. Some eat zebras, buffalo, and even lions! To kill large **prey**, the crocodile drags them under water. Then it spins around and tears off bits of flesh.

◄ An American alligator opens wide.

prey animal that is killed and eaten by other animals

Breeding

Colour attractions

Lizards use skin colours to attract a partner for breeding.

The **marine** iguana is normally dark in colour. During the mating season, it comes out in red spots. This means: "I am ready to mate."

Most of the time reptiles live alone. But they have many ways of finding and attracting a partner.

Lizard partners

Male lizards often fight during the **breeding** season. Some geckos chirp and "bark" to attract a female. Others bob up and down for hours as if they are doing press-ups!

Snake breeding

Snakes attract each other by giving off a special smell through their skin.

▼ The male Texas banded gecko will attract a mate by hitting her gently with his tail as he licks her.

Eggs and young

Most snakes lay eggs, but some give birth to fully-formed young.

Garter snakes live in North America. When spring comes, they **mate** in a big tangle of lots of snakes. A month or two later, the females each give birth to up to 60 live young.

Perfect partners

The male Nile crocodile calls a female by thrashing his strong tail through the water.

Male alligators, like the one above, open their mouths and roar to attract a female.

◀ These garter snakes will mate and then slither away.

mate when a male and female animal come together to produce young

Whiptail lizards
(below) are very
unusual. The
females can
produce young
without **mating**.
They do not need
the male. How
amazing is that?

Turtle young

All turtles and tortoises lay their eggs on land.
Most sea turtles return to the same beach where
they were born. Here the females drag
themselves on to the shore. They dig a hole in
the sand and lay around 100 eggs.

Very few young turtles **survive** long enough to
race back to the sea. This is because birds,
crabs, and fish catch and eat them.

▼Tiny loggerhead turtles rush
down to the safety of the sea
after hatching.

Crocodile parents

Not many reptiles are caring parents. Most leave their young to grow up on their own.

Female **crocodilians** do care for their young. They guard them for weeks from hungry **predators**. Sometimes the mother gently carries her young around in her mouth. Even so, only around 2 per cent of the eggs survive to be adults.

Breaking out

Some young reptiles have an "egg tooth". This is a special, sharp tooth they use to cut themselves out of the egg. The sea turtle below is hatching out from its egg.

mate when a male and female animal come together to produce young

Defence

Many reptiles have to defend themselves against **predators** that want to eat them.

Poisonous snakes

One way of defending yourself is with poison. Less than one third of the world's snakes are poisonous. They use their poison to defend themselves as well as to kill their **prey**.

The king cobra is poisonous. With one bite it can produce enough poison to kill ten adult humans.

Fangs

Some snakes have **fangs** that fold away in the roof of their mouth. To bite, the fangs spring forward. Poison squirts down the fangs into the prey. Look at the scary fangs of the Eastern diamondback snake below.

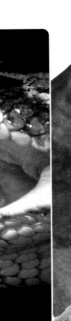

▼ This is a Gila monster. Its bright colours say "keep away!"

fang long, sharp tooth that injects poison into prey

Deadly lizards

The Gila monster is one of only two **species** of lizard in the world with poison. It lives in the western part of North America.

Its thick body is patterned with black and pink (or yellow) bands. These bright colours are a warning to predators that it has a poisonous bite.

Dangerous mambas

The very fast black mamba (below) is one of the deadliest snakes of all.

In just one bite it makes enough poison to kill 260 people. A bite from this snake can kill a human within one hour.

species type of living animal or plant

Keeping still

Chameleons have eyes that can swivel and see all around. The two eyes can look in different directions at the same time. This is useful for spotting predators – and for finding prey.

Camouflage

Chameleons are amazing lizards. They can change colour to blend in with their surroundings. Their mood and temperature also affect their colour.

This blending in, or **camouflage**, helps hide chameleons from **predators**. It makes them harder to spot. It also means they can creep up on their **prey** without being seen.

▼ This veiled chameleon blends in well with the green leaves around it.

camouflage colours and patterns that match the background

◄ Can you see the head of the desert adder in the sand?

Spiny protection

The armadillo girdle-tailed lizard lives in South Africa. It has sharp, spiny **scales** on its tail. When it is scared it rolls into a ball with its tail in its mouth. This makes it hard for a predator to attack.

Blending colours

Many animals eat snakes. Forest snakes are often green, brown, or spotted. They blend in well against leaves and tree trunks. Predators have to look hard to find them.

Nothing but sand

The desert adder digs itself in the sand so only its head sticks out. Its head is the colour of sand, so there is nothing to see!

Stink bomb

The freshwater musk turtle (above) has another name: stinkpot. It lets out a bad-smelling liquid when it is scared. Most predators back off and leave it alone.

Special tricks

Reptiles have many different ways to protect themselves from **predators**.

To stop being eaten, the Australian frilled lizard tries to look scary. It opens its mouth, shows its teeth, and waves its tongue. It also hisses and puffs out a big frill around its neck. It is enough to scare off most attackers.

▲ A frilled lizard opens its frill to scare off predators.

More tricks

The West Indian wood snake has a different way of putting off predators. If frightened, it pretends to be dead. It even makes a smell like rotting flesh. If that does not work, the snake fills its eyes with blood and bleeds from the mouth!

Rattlesnakes just shake their tails. The rattling noise may help keep predators away. The rattle is hollow inside and makes a buzzing sound when the snake moves it.

Blood eyes

The Texas horned lizard (below) is only about the length of a pencil. It has a very scary trick. When scared, it shoots blood into the face of a predator. The blood comes from in and around its eyes.

Weird and wonderful

Komodo dragons are huge lizards. They have sharp claws and a long, powerful tail. They live on islands in South-East Asia.

In one meal, the Komodo dragon can eat nearly its own weight in meat! One dragon was seen eating a whole pig in just 17 minutes. That is like someone eating 600 hamburgers at once!

Fact or fiction?

The Komodo dragon is the world's heaviest lizard. Even so, some people think that an even larger lizard may exist. There are stories of huge lizards living in the **rainforests** of New Guinea (shown below).

> ▶ These are Komodo dragons. They rip up their prey before swallowing it in big pieces.

rainforest forest that grows in warm parts of the world where there is a lot of rainfall

Deadly bite

The bite of a Komodo dragon is deadly. These lizards eat rotting flesh and have a lot of dangerous **bacteria** in their mouths. When they bite their **prey**, these bacteria get into the wound.

The prey soon becomes sick and dies of blood poisoning. Then the dragons go and eat its body.

Big brother?

A huge lizard once lived in Australia. It was like a giant Komodo dragon and was called *Megalania*. Its skull alone (shown below) was as long as a large suitcase.

bacteria very small living things that can cause disease

Super croc

Seventy million years ago, huge crocodiles walked the Earth. They were the size of a bus and probably hunted **dinosaurs**. They may have lived in swamps in what is now Texas, USA.

Amazing crocodiles

One of the strange things about crocodiles is that they heal very quickly if they get hurt.

Crocodiles often get into fights and sometimes tear off legs or tails. Even if they get ripped open, their bodies soon repair. Scientists think there may be something special in the crocodile's blood that helps it to heal so quickly.

► The Nile crocodile has very sharp teeth, but the crocodile bird is not afraid of them.

dinosaur group of large reptiles that lived millions of years ago

Best of friends

Most animals keep away from crocodiles. Yet one animal steps right into its open jaws.

When Nile crocodiles sunbathe they open their mouths wide. Along comes a crocodile bird and in it hops! The bird picks bits of meat from the crocodile's teeth. It gets a free dinner and the crocodile gets a free dentist.

▼ This crocodile is a called a mugger. The word "mugger" means "water monster". These reptiles live in India and Sri Lanka.

Killer saltie

In December 2003, two teenage boys clung to a tree for 22 hours in an Australian swamp. A saltwater crocodile had already killed their friend. It stayed under the tree all night until help came for the boys.

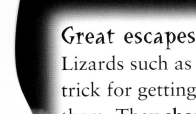

Great escapes

Lizards such as geckos and skinks have a great trick for getting away from anything that grabs them. They **shed** their tail and run. The tail twitches on the ground for a while to confuse the **predator**. Then the lizard makes its escape.

Amazingly, the lizard will grow a new tail in just a few months.

Mini reptile

It is easy to hide if you are tiny. The Virgin Island gecko is about as long as a paperclip (the photo below has made the geckos bigger so you can see them easily).

Magic feet

Another useful trick for escaping predators is to run upside-down. Geckos have special, sticky feet. They can run up glass or upside-down on ceilings.

The basilisk lizard from South America can run on its two back legs. Amazingly, it can also run on water because of its special feet. These trap air under them, and keep the lizard from sinking.

Zebra tail

The zebra-tailed lizard (below) has a black-and-white pattern under its tail. It waves this at a predator to put it in a kind of **trance**. While the predator still feels confused, the lizard escapes.

▼ Basilisk lizards can run up to 40 metres (over 130 feet) across a pond. But if this one stops running it will sink.

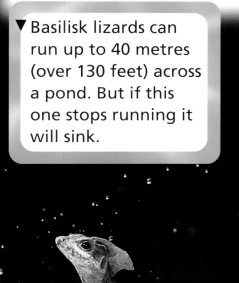

trance special state that is like being asleep

Pets go wild

The Everglades in Florida, USA, has a problem. Many pet reptiles have been let go or have escaped there.

More than 1000 snakes escaped into the wild after Hurricane Andrew in 1992. People have seen huge pythons living in Florida's swamps (pythons normally live in Asia). If the pythons manage to **breed** successfully, they could be a threat to the wildlife there.

Going home

Some turtles have powers we do not understand. They can travel for thousands of kilometres across the sea. They find their way back to the beach where they were born to lay their own eggs.

breed produce young

Going travelling

The Everglades are home to alligators. They live in the swamps, ponds, and canals there.

In south Florida alligators move around a lot and can appear in strange places. They travel about in search of food. Or they look for water if their waterholes dry up. People sometimes find them in their swimming pools or on golf courses.

On the move

In the 1930s a scientist was on a ship in the Pacific Ocean. He saw a strange line in the water. It was a mass of sea snakes moving together. There were millions of them and the line stretched for 96 kilometres (60 miles).

▼ Can you see the crocodiles on this golf course in South Africa?

▲ These are yellow-bellied sea snakes. They sometimes get washed up on to beaches.

Reptiles in danger

Taken as pets

Thousands of wild reptiles are caught each year and sold as pets. Many of these animals die because their owners do not know how to look after them.

Many reptiles are **endangered.** Humans are damaging or destroying the places where they live. Many reptiles are taken from the wild and sold as pets.

Threats to turtles

Sea turtles are in special danger. When they come up to breathe they are easy to catch. Egg collectors also take turtle eggs from the shore.

▶ This is an Orinoco crocodile. These crocodiles may not **survive** the next few years.

　endangered in danger of dying out

Crocodiles in danger

The Orinoco crocodile is South America's largest **predator**. Between the 1930s and 1960s people hunted this crocodile for its skin. The crocodile nearly died out.

Today, there are probably only a few hundred Orinoco crocodiles left in the wild. People still hunt them for their meat and eggs even though this is now against the law.

Skin hunters

Water monitor lizards are hunted in South-East Asia. People kill more than 1 million monitors each year. They use their skin, to make things like bags, shoes, and watchstraps.

▼ The painted terrapin is endangered in South-East Asia because people eat its eggs.

Reptile attack

Snakes and crocodiles can attack people. It can be dangerous to go swimming or walking in places like Tavares, Florida (see below) where these animals live. But this is not a reason to kill these reptiles.

Reptiles and us

Reptiles have a hard time. Over the years we have killed millions of them for their meat, eggs, skins, and shells. Sometimes we kill them simply because we are scared of them.

Nowhere to go

We are also destroying the places where reptiles live with our rubbish and **pollution**. We build roads and houses by lakes, rivers, and seas. This means reptiles have to find somewhere else to live.

▶ A loggerhead turtle is returned to the sea. It has been given a health check and is ready to go free again.

pollution damage caused by chemicals, fumes, and rubbish

The good news

It is not all bad news, though. There are many projects around the world to protect reptiles.

The Australian pygmy blue-tongued skink disappeared for 33 years. It turned up again in 1992 and is now doing well.

Reptiles have been on Earth for hundreds of millions of years. We need to keep it that way.

High fashion

Python skin is fashionable. People use it to make bags, belts, and skirts. The python skins below are on sale in Cambodia. Pythons from the wild are often killed for their skins.

Find out more

Websites

BBC Nature
Website full of pictures and information about nature.
www.bbc.co.uk/ nature/animals

Backyard Nature
Website with information on identifying common reptiles.
www.backyard nature.net/ 2reptile.htm

More links
Lots of great links to many more websites on reptiles.
www.wc4.org/ reptiles_snakes .htm

Classifying Living Things: Reptiles, Louise and Richard Spilsbury (Heinemann Library, 2002)
Everything Reptile (Kid's FAQs), Cherie Winner (Northword Press, 2004)
Reptile (Eyewitness Guides), Colin McCarthy (Dorling Kindersley, 1998)

World wide web

To find out more about reptiles you can search the Internet. Use keywords like these:
- "Nile crocodile"
- oldest +tortoise
- "poisonous snakes"

You can find your own keywords by using words from this book. The search tips on page 53 will help you find useful websites.

Search tips

There are billions of pages on the Internet. It can be difficult to find exactly what you are looking for. These tips will help you find useful websites more quickly:

- Know what you want to find out about
- Use simple keywords
- Use two to six keywords in a search
- Only use names of people, places, or things
- Put double quote marks around words that go together, for example "monitor lizard"

Where to search

Search engine
A search engine looks through millions of website pages. It lists all the sites that match the words in the search box. You will find the best matches are at the top of the list on the first page.

Search directory
A person instead of a computer has sorted a search directory. You can search by keyword or subject and browse through the different sites. It is like looking through books on a library shelf.

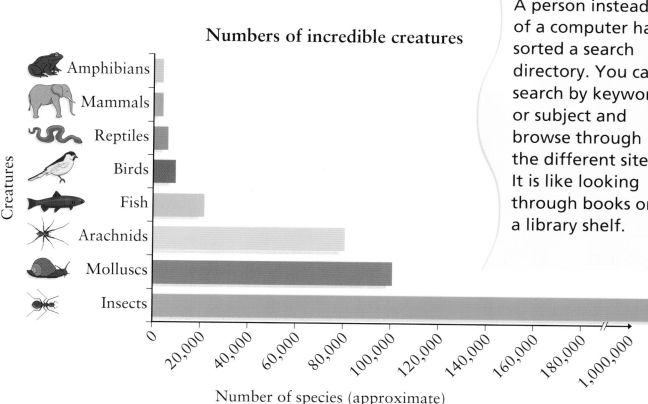

Numbers of incredible creatures

Creatures: Amphibians, Mammals, Reptiles, Birds, Fish, Arachnids, Molluscs, Insects

Number of species (approximate)

Glossary

acid type of liquid that can be strong enough to break down tough materials

bacteria very small living things that can cause disease

bask lie in the sun to warm up

breed produce young

burrow make a hole in the ground

camouflage colours and patterns that match the background

carnivore animal that eats meat

cold-blooded having a body temperature that depends on the temperature of the surroundings

crocodilian reptile such as a crocodile, alligator, caiman, and gharial

digest break down food so it can be used in the body

digestion breaking down food in the body after eating

dinosaur group of large reptiles that lived millions of years ago

endangered in danger of dying out

evolve change very slowly over time

fang long, sharp tooth that injects poison into prey

flexible able to move or bend very easily

gills delicate, feathery structures that allow some animals to breathe under water

herbivore animal that only eats plants – a vegetarian

marine to do with the sea

mate when a male and female animal come together to produce young

oxygen one of the gases in air and water that all living things need

pollution damage caused by chemicals, fumes, and rubbish

predator animal that kills and eats other animals

prey animal that is killed and eaten by other animals

rainforest forest that grows in warm parts of the world where there is a lot of rainfall

scales small, horny, or bony plates that protect the skin on reptiles and fish

shed get rid of, or lose

snout nose

species type of living animal
  or plant
survive stay alive despite danger
  and difficulties
survivor someone or something
  that has stayed alive
trance special state that is like
  being asleep
vertebrate animal with a backbone

Index

Titles in the *Freestyle Express*: *Incredible Creatures* series include:

Hardback: 1844 434516

Hardback: 1844 434524

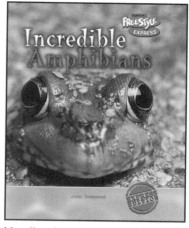

Hardback: 1844 434532

Hardback: 1844 434540

Hardback: 1844 434761

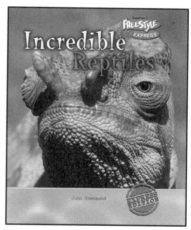

Hardback: 1844 43477X

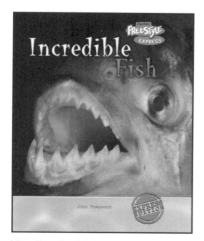

Hardback: 1844 435172

Hardback: 1844 435180

Find out about other Freestyle Express titles on our website www.raintreepublishers.co.uk